The Conversion of Ratisbonne

The Conversion of Ratisbonne

Narratives of Alphonse Ratisbonne and Baron Theodore de Bussieres

Roman Catholic Books
P.O. Box 2286 • Fort Collins, CO 80522

THE CONVERSION OF RATISBONNE

This edited edition copyright ©2000 by Roman Catholic Books

ISBN 0-912141-88-3

CONTRIBUTORS

Emmanuel Lemuel McCall, Sr. is associate secretary in the Department of Work with National Baptists of the Southern Baptist Home Mission Board. He is a native of Sharon, Pennsylvania, a graduate of the University of Louisville, and a graduate of Southern Baptist Theological Seminary, Louisville, Kentucky. He also attended Simmons University in Louisville. He has held several pastorates and served ten years as a college professor.

Robert H. Wilson is pastor of St. John Baptist Church, Dallas, Texas. He is a native of Columbia, South Carolina. He is a graduate of Benedict College, Columbia, South Carolina, and has held a number of pastorates. He has traveled extensively serving churches, ministerial conferences, and colleges as evangelist and lecturer. Foreign travel includes Western Europe, the Holy Land, and Africa. In his present pastorate the church has shown remarkable growth in recent years.

Percy A. Carter, Jr. is pastor of Hosack Street Baptist Church, Columbus, Ohio. He is a native of Hampton, Virginia and a graduate of Virginia Union University in Richmond, Virginia, Andover Newton Theological School, and Boston University School of Theology. He also attended Harvard University and Brown University, and was a Danforth Special Fellow at Brown. He has held a number of pastorates, been a Chaplain Major in the Air Force Reserve, and is active in civic affairs.

Nelson H. Smith, Jr. is pastor of New Pilgrim Baptist Church, Birmingham, Alabama. A native of Brewton, Alabama, he is a graduate of Selma University, has held a number of pastorates, and is active in civic affairs. He is the son of a pastor, his father having served churches in Alabama and Mississippi for more than 50 years.

Charles E. Boddie is president of American Baptist Theological Seminary, Nashville, Tennessee. A person of superior ability and deep devotion to the Lord, he is very well known, not only in his own denomination where he is very active, but throughout the South.

Edward V. Hill is pastor of Mount Zion Missionary Baptist Church, Los Angeles, California. A native of Texas, he is active in civic, political, and national affairs, in addition to being very active in his denomination.

Manuel L. Scott is pastor of Calvary Baptist Church, Los Angeles, California. He is a popular speaker at Southern Baptist state evangelistic conferences and at other meetings, in addition to being active in his denomination. A previous book for Broadman is *From a Black Brother,* 1971.

TABLE OF CONTENTS

Foreword 7

From the Preface to the Original English Edition 9

Narrative of Baron Theodore de Bussieres 21

Narrative of Marie-Alphonse Ratisbonne 51

Epilogue 75

Appendix 77

Decree Verifying and Accrediting the Miracle 83

The Conversion of Ratisbonne

RATISBONNE, MARIE ALPHONSE, co-founder of the Congregation of Notre Dame de Sion and Fathers of Sion; b. Strasbourg, France, May 1, 1814; d. Ain Karim, Palestine, May 6, 1884. Alphonse, the ninth child of the most important Jewish family in Alsace, became a lawyer and banker. Like his brother Theodore he was eager to aid his fellow Jews. So bitterly anti-Christian was he that he was unable to forgive Theodore for becoming a Catholic in 1827. But on his way to the East, he visited Rome, where he was suddenly converted after a vision of the Blessed Virgin Mary in the Church of St. Andrea delle Fratte (Jan. 20, 1842). At the time of his baptism (Jan. 31), he took the name Marie. A few months later he joined the Jesuits. After his ordination (1848) he received permission to leave the Society of Jesus and collaborate with his brother in working for the conversion of the Jews. He collaborated with Theodore in founding their two congregations. In 1855 he went to Palestine, where he spent the remainder of his life laboring to convert Jews and Moslems. He established for the Sisters of Sion the Ecce Homo monastery (1856) and later opened two orphanages.

—*The New Catholic Encyclopedia*

Foreword

These are the first-hand accounts of the 1842 conversion of Alphonse Ratisbonne, declared by the Church to be the direct result of the miraculous intervention of Mary. They should be of more than antiquarian interest to modern readers because Ratisbonne was himself, until the moment of his conversion, very much a modern.

He was above all worldly. Although his family was nominally Jewish, he had nearly as much contempt for traditional Jewish belief and practice as he had for the Catholic Church. He was active in charitable work on behalf of poor Jews, but only with the goal of helping them materially. Alphonse Ratisbonne despised all religion as foolish superstition and an obstacle to human progress. For the Catholic Church, however, he had a particular, implacable hatred because his elder brother Theodore had not only converted, but had been ordained a priest in 1830.

His parents died when he was young, but his paternal uncle, a wealthy and influential banker of Strasbourg, the capital of Alsace, became a second father to him and sent him to study law in Paris. There he enjoyed fashionable society and sophisticated entertainments. He was made a partner in his uncle's bank in January 1842.

The trappings of the story—carriages and calling cards—are of the 19th century, but substitute expensive automobiles for the carriages, and you have the complete worldly, sophisticated man of the present day, wealthy, educated and pampered. It would be difficult to imagine a less likely person to see the Blessed Virgin Mary in an unprepossessing Roman church. When he said he had seen her, when he requested Baptism, he acted against his every worldly interest, sacrificing wealth, family, friends and the certain prospect of a brilliant career. In the world's terms—in his own terms up until the minute he saw her—he had everything to lose, and nothing to gain.

The account of Ratisbonne's baptism at the end of Baron de Bussieres' narrative may or may not be written by de Bussieres. In the portion that is clearly his, he speaks of himself only in the first person; but it may well be that he turned to the third person at the end as a literary device, to make the baptism scene more lofty and august.

From the Preface to the Original English Edition

We have given in this volume a literal translation of the original accounts of the conversion of Alphonse Ratisbonne. The attempt to construct an independent narrative would be presumptuous in itself, and would lose the simple force and freshness of these documents. Those who know the scrupulous and almost suspicious care with which the pretensions of any alleged miracle are tested at Rome will feel the value of the decree of the Cardinal-Vicar [epilogue, p. 73]. Baron de Bussieres prefaced his first edition with a declaration that he claimed for his narrative only the assent that may be granted to any ordinary statement, resting on human evidence alone; this decree has raised the conversion of Ratisbonne to the position of an accredited miracle.

It is both sad and strange to observe the air of superb disdain with which miracles such as this are set aside, even by those who seem close to the Catholic Church, and who profess to accept the miracles of Holy Scripture on their own evidence, and to be familiar with the laws of moral reasoning.

And yet, surely, those who reject this miracle as an imposture or a delusion should feel bound to show how it lacks the criteria of a true miracle. We may assume they would be unwilling to affirm that the power of working miracles was restrained within the limits of the apostolic age; they know that this hypothesis is fatal to historical Christianity, and belies the promise of its inspired records. Nor will they say that a miracle is so improbable a thing that no amount of testimony can render it credible; they know well that with this view they could hardly rescue the miracles of the Gospels from the hands of unbelievers.

They must rest their rejection on one of these grounds: either they regard the evidence for this particular miracle as insufficient or untrustworthy, or they shrink from doctrines and practices this miracle implies.

Yet they freely admit that objections to any revelation from God, as distinguished from objections to its evidence, are frivolous. It is not up to them to set aside credible testimony to a miracle, simply because that miracle carries with it theological consequences which they deem at variance with the general scheme of religion. The only question they can logically entertain is the evidence for this particular miracle—the apparition of the Blessed Virgin to Alphonse Ratisbonne in the Church of St. Andrea at Rome.

And if we weigh the character of the witness and his competency; the improbability of his being deceived or wishing to deceive; the simple fact of the entire change wrought upon him in a moment, in the conversion of his heart and the illumination of his mind; the consequences of his testimony to himself; and the years which have tested his sincerity and stability—if we weigh all these circumstances, we may ask whether it is possible to decline to receive his testimony on any grounds that would not excuse the Jews who dwelt at Damascus for refusing to credit the conversion of Saul of Tarsus, and Festus for deeming him mad.

It bears repeating that those who feel that there is no antecedent improbability in the occurrence of miracles—that the later miracles cannot be discredited on *a priori* grounds without shaking the credit of those of the Gospels—are bound to justify their rejection of this miracle by impeaching its evidence. This is the only issue a Christian can properly raise; and that testimony cannot be trivial or indifferent which the Church has stamped with the seal of its acceptance.

Equally worth considering are some observations of Cardinal Wiseman, in his review of a pamphlet entitled *A Voice from Rome*:

> In proof that the Blessed Virgin is worshipped as the mother of mercies, temporal and spiritual, the author before us appeals to the Baron de Bussieres' account of M. Ratisbonne's conversion from Judaism, "which he distinctly attributes to the immediate operation of the Virgin Mary, for he relates that it was effected by her actual appearance to him." Now, what is meant to be granted, and what is meant to be doubted here, we do not know. We suppose that no one doubts that M. Ratisbonne, from a Jew, did become a Catholic, and has become a religious, having abandoned home and friends, and given up a long-cherished alliance. Anyone might as well deny that Sir R. Peel is Prime Minister. That he went into the Church of St. Andrea a Jew, and came out a Christian, is attested upon evidence as certain as any fact can well be—that of trustworthy and honest men, who saw him and spoke with him before and after. For the change something must account.
>
> That it was a true conversion from Judaism to Christianity, with great temporal sacrifices, is clear; and such a conversion must be the work of divine grace. How the grace was communicated is the only question. The only witness can be the convert. He tells us that it was through an apparition of the Mother of God, who instructed him in the mysteries of our holy reli-

gion. Are we to believe that a person is chosen by Providence as an object of a singular act of grace, at the moment that he devises and tells an abominable falsehood, to rob God of the glory of it and give it to another by feigning a vision of the Blessed Virgin? What does the author of *A Voice from Rome* mean to throw doubt on? On the apparition, as for such a purpose impossible? Or on the consequences drawn from it? Surely not on the latter; for if the vision was true, it is right to consider the Blessed Mother not as the source, but as the channel of a great spiritual mercy.

If he wishes to insinuate that it would be derogatory to God's honor, or incompatible with His revealed doctrines, to believe such a mode of communicating grace and religious instruction possible, and that the whole must consequently be considered a figment or a delusion, we will, in answer, relate a similar story, in which not a Jew, but a bishop, was the party. We have this story on the best authority.

The person to whom we allude was a young man of singular piety and virtue. Left young an orphan, he devoted his youth to study in a celebrated university. There his devotion to learning was surpassed only by the purity and innocence of his life, which stood the test of severe trials, and escaped the snares laid for him by profligate companions, jealous of his virtue. Having made himself master of all profane learning, he entered on a course of sacred studies under the most celebrated professor of the day, and soon made considerable progress. While yet young, he was put into holy orders, and even named bishop, before he considered himself well enough grounded in theology—probably

Preface to the Original English Edition

his humility led him to exaggerate his deficiencies.

He found himself quite unequal to the task of preaching, and on the eve of his first sermon he lay sleepless in anxiety. Suddenly he saw before him a venerable figure of an old man whose countenance, attitude and clothing suggested great dignity, but who also appeared most gracious and affable. Terrified at this appearance, the young man leaped from his bed, and respectfully asked who he was, and for what purpose he had come. The old man gently replied that he had come to calm his doubts and solve his difficulties. Then he pointed to the other side of the room, where the young man saw a lady of great majesty, and of more than human beauty, so resplendent that his eyes could not bear the brightness of the vision—he was obliged to look down in reverential awe. Thus he listened to the conversation of these two heavenly beings, which fully instructed him on the subjects that had caused him anxiety, and at the same time informed him who his gracious visitors were. For the lady, addressing the other by the name of the Evangelist John, asked him to instruct the youth in the mystery of heavenly piety; and he replied that he was ready to do this, to please the Mother of his Lord, seeing that she wished it. And he did so.

This is our counterpart to the narrative objected to by *A Voice from Rome*, regarding M. Ratisbonne's conversion. Now, before giving the name of our authority for this wonderful history, or of the person to whom it refers, we beg the reader to say to what church or religion he considers either the writer or the subject of this anecdote belongs. Could he believe us, if we told him that it happened to Archbishop Laud? Or that we had transcribed it as it was told by some Anglican clergyman? Certainly not. The idea of a Protestant bishop learning his faith from a vision of the Blessed Virgin would be deemed repugnant to every principle and feeling of the religion. But were we to tell the reader that the bishop spoken of was Alphonsus Liguori, or even St. Charles, and the narrator an Italian monk or priest, he would at once allow that such an account, from such a pen, concerning such a person, was perfectly consistent with the principles of both. Although, as a Protestant, he might declare that he did not believe the story, he would acknowledge that it did not surprise him to find it in such a place. It must, then, be a Catholic, and not a Protestant, who thought or said he saw such a vision; and it must be a Catholic, and not a Protestant, who has recorded it, as believing it. And so it was. The bishop who thus learned his faith was St. Gregory Thaumaturgus, only a little more than two hundred years after Christ; and the recorder of the vision is the brother of the great St. Basil, St. Gregory, Bishop of Nyssa. This would have been a nice anecdote for our ancient note-taker upon the doctrines of the Catholics.

The real reason miracles such as this are rejected with scorn, or passed by with indifference, is not their antecedent improbability or the inadequacy of their evidence. It is that they imply the position and power of the blessed Mother of God. The Protestant cannot endure that glad and graceful vision of the Mother of Divine Grace. It is an offence to him. It is something so intolerable to him that, in his antipathy, he forgets all rules of moral reasoning. His conceptions and definitions become confused, neutralizing the positive evidence that the Church which discloses this vision is alone of God.

And yet, waiving hypothetically what we can never forget in fact, that clear voice of the Church which is the Catholic's warrant of faith, why should it be thought a thing so violently incredible that the Mother of God should occupy the position and exercise the power ascribed to her by the Church? Surely there can be no natural and necessary improbability in that which East and West combine to affirm. Except in the minds of a modern and very small section of the nominally Christian world, there has never been any consciousness of an incompatibility between her assigned office and the Gospel. Her glories and prerogatives, as Mother of Christians and a special channel of grace, have not shocked the wisest and holiest sons of the Church.

Nor can those who rightly ascribe so tremendous an influence to Eve over the destinies of our race rightfully shrink from the range of power attributed by the Church to the counterpart of Eve. It cannot, surely, be a gratuitous fancy to see in the effects of the unbelief and disobedience of the mother of all the living, in the order of nature, a hint of the efficacy of the faith and obedience of the mother of all the living, in the order of grace.

But let us observe here that the miraculous element in the conversion narrated in this book is simply the apparition of the Mother of God, and not her intercessory power. The Catholic regards that power as a supernatural fact, a law of the spiritual kingdom. He needs no miracle to teach it to him. No number or splendor of miracles could increase his faith in it. They would only verify what he already knows. Such a miracle as this might excite his faith, but it would not be its cause. He sees the office and the prerogatives of the Blessed Virgin involved in the fact of the Incarnation. *Mary, of whom was born Jesus Christ*—he needs no more. Mary, Mother of God; Mary, bequeathed to us as our mother from the Cross: the divine maternity includes and implies all. Her glories and her mighty power are only its natural consequences, and its fitting adornment.

Is he reminded of the absence of express commands to seek her intercession? He feels that he has the command of that same Spirit by whose inspiration Scripture was written. For the Church always says, *it has thus seemed good to the Holy Ghost and to us*. He would remind the objector that the relation in which the Mother of God stands to us being known, the duty of religious regard to her arises out of that relation itself, and is an obligation of reason, binding as soon as that relation is known. It is our duty as well as our privilege to seek the intercession of those who have power with God; and he would call on the objector to produce some prohibition of so natural an exercise of that privilege.

But then, to invoke the Blessed Mother, to imagine that she can hear our cry and turn on us her pitying eyes—it is this which is deemed so absurd as to need no refutation. As if the charge of absurdity did not recoil on those who impose on the world unseen the laws of space and time and the like which rule this world that is seen! They limit the range of the perceptions of the blessed by the laws of man's bodily senses, senses which are only the spirit's points of contact with the material world. Surely it is both shallow and unscientific to reason from the sense of this body to the powers and perceptions of the saints who reign with Christ. True, we do not know precisely how the saints hear our invocations. It is enough to say that we can imagine many ways in which they may know the desires of our hearts.

Still there is a jealousy, honorable in its motive, most unwise in its conclusions, that our recourse to the Blessed Mother of Christians does in some way interfere with the simplicity of our trust in Jesus Christ. It is impossible for those who are outside to understand the practical and ever-present safeguards of the Catholic from all error, from all excess. They cannot know, for instance, the effect of the Mass in regulating all his language and thoughts, or how impossible it is that this perception of the greatness of the powers God does communicate to the creature should lessen the greatness or dim the glory of those which are incommunicable. Surely it should suffice to affirm that the sole mediatorship of the Son of God is the very foundation of all Catholic theology and practice. Like the weakness of man and the might of grace, it is a law of the spiritual order, everywhere felt, everywhere presupposed, everywhere taken for granted, underlying every statement, directing every prayer. But the intercession of the Blessed Virgin and of the saints cannot be so stated as to clash with this oneness of mediation. They cannot ask otherwise than in accordance with His will, or apart from His great pleading. It is upon the altar which is before the throne of God that the prayers of all the saints are offered in St. John's vision.

Now, this is ever present to the Catholic. However much he may ask of our Blessed Mother—and he does ask much—the principle of his asking and the law of its interpretation are, *Tu da, per precata dulcisona*—by thy sweet prevailing prayer. It cannot be otherwise to him. He is never even tempted to confuse the creatures with the Creator, to mistake the streams for the source.

But it is not the illumination of the mind that is needed to bring back the strayed sheep to the fold. It is the attraction of the heart and the bending of the will, and these are the work of God alone. If those who doubt and object would only meditate a while on the solitary prerogative of Mary, and on the intensity of the mutual love that must bind together that Son and that mother—if they would only look at her revealed position from the Church's point of view, with all those limitations and checks and safeguards of which they can have no idea—if they would do this, not with the hard, cold gaze of the intellect, but with a loving, docile heart—the objections which now hang like clouds before their souls' eyes would melt away of themselves, leaving no trace. To such men we say, in all affection, if you must reason before you believe, remember the laws that control all moral reasoning. Remember that no number of even irreducible objections carry weight against direct and positive evidence; remember that those who, like St. Bernard, St. Anselm, St. Bonaventura, St. Alphonsus, have been most devoted to Mary have spoken of Jesus Christ with the tongues of angels rather than of men; and pray.

And as you gaze, you will see how the Mother of Jesus Christ is the Mother of His mystical body as well. As you consider the meaning of the words, *Behold the handmaid of the Lord*, you will understand that it is a mighty prayer to say, *Behold, O Lord, how I am your servant, and the son of your handmaid*.

An apology is due our Catholic readers for the length to which these remarks have extended. You can hardly grasp the reality of the difficulty which Protestants feel in the intercession of the Blessed Virgin and of the saints. You can scarcely believe that men who believe the mystery of the In-

Preface to the Original English Edition

carnation can really be confused about something so consonant with that faith as the Christian's recourse to the prayers of all the saints. To you the miracle related here is quite natural and in keeping—wonderful indeed, but still what you are prepared to expect from the Mother of mercy.

To you all Scripture speaks of her, in type and in figure, in prophecy and in promise. To you the Incarnation is unintelligible apart from her. You know that as you have loved Jesus Christ more, you have felt for her whom He loved best on earth—whom He must delight to honor in Heaven—a truer, deeper, more loyal and more trustful love. You know that as your devotion to the Mother of God has gathered strength, you have known and loved her Son with a less reserved love.

This narrative is of conversion, of Mary's tender pity towards those who know her not. How can we better express our thankfulness for this instance of her compassion than by praying for those to whom that very compassion is an offence and a hindrance? Let us pray for those who, from amid their gathering gloom, are casting wistful, timid looks towards the one unwavering light, that God's grace may still lead them on, and gently clear their way through their thorny objections, until it

Brings them under Mary's smile
And Peter's royal feet.

—*Rev. W. Lockhart*

THE NARRATIVE OF BARON THEODORE DE BUSSIERES

Towards the close of the autumn of 1841, a young man, connected with a distinguished family at Strasbourg, arrived at Naples. He was on his way to the East, in quest of health and pleasure, but he had left his native city with regret, for he left there an attractive, gentle girl whom he loved very much, and in whom his heart had stored up its rich treasure of hope. She was his own niece; but mutual affection, no less than family reasons, had determined their union.

Alphonse Ratisbonne was a Jew; he seemed destined to a brilliant position in the world, and had resolved to devote himself to the assistance of the poor among his co-religionists. His thoughts and aspirations all revolved around this one high purpose, and his wrath kindled at everything that reminded him of the curse upon the descendants of Jacob. Fifteen years before the time of which I am speaking, and while he was yet a child, a bitter tragedy had struck his beloved family. Theodore Ratisbonne, his brother, became a Catholic and received holy orders. Alphonse's anger at this treachery, and his hatred of the Church, had deepened as the years had gone by; and he studiously encouraged the deadly resentment of the rest of his family.

The blue sky of Naples could not make him forget the East, the object of his journey, or the joys that awaited him upon his return. Only a few months remained, and he had still to visit Sicily, Malta and Constantinople. The summer of 1842 was to restore him to his home, and to witness a union which would fix his position in life, and assure his perfect happiness. It was time to be going.

The Conversion of Ratisbonne

So he went out one morning to reserve his place on the steamer for Palermo. On his way it struck him that he had not seen Rome; that if he returned to Strasbourg, and married, and became involved in the cares of business, there was little likelihood of his ever revisiting Italy. Under the influence of this sudden thought he turned aside into the stage office and reserved his place. Within three days he found himself in Rome.

His stay was to be very short. His plans were all made; in a fortnight he would return to Naples. In vain the Eternal City displayed her wonders before him; he could not spare a day more. He set to work like a true tourist, visiting ruins, churches and galleries and crowding his memory with a confused medley of impressions. He was eager to have done with this city, to which he had been drawn by an unaccountable fascination rather than by an intelligent curiosity.

And now he has finished his rounds. It is Saturday, January 15. He starts for Naples tomorrow, but he must pay a farewell visit to an old friend. Gustave de Bussieres, my brother, had been his schoolfellow and they had kept up their early friendship in spite of the antagonism of their religious opinions. My brother is a very zealous Protestant, of the sect of the Pietists. He had made many attempts to win over the young Jew, but their discussions usually wound up with two expressions which are typical of the position and temper of the disputants. "Fanatical Protestant!" shouted the one; "Callous Jew!" retorted the other.

Ratisbonne did not find my brother at home, and so he came on to my house. He had resolved not to come in; he would merely leave a calling card in farewell. Chance, or perhaps Providence, ordered it so that his knock was answered by an Italian servant who misunderstood him—and introduced him, to his great annoyance, into the drawing room.

We had met only once, at my brother's, and notwithstanding all my efforts, I had failed to obtain from Ratisbonne anything beyond the cold civility of a well-bred man. However, he was Gustave's friend and the brother of my own dear friend, the Abbe Maria Theodore Ratisbonne, and so I received him cordially. I talked to him of the wonders around him, and gradually elicited his impressions of Rome.

"A rather odd thing happened to me the other day," said he, in passing. "While I was looking over the Church of Aracoeli on the Capitol, I felt myself suddenly seized with an emotion for which I could assign no cause. The guide, seeing my agitation, asked me what was the matter, and whether I would like to go out in the open air. He said he had often seen visitors similarly affected."

I suppose my eyes seemed to say to him, *You will be a Catholic*, for he went on to say, markedly, that this emotion was not at all specifically Christian, but purely religious, in the most general sense of the word.

"Besides," he continued, "as I came down from the Capitol a melancholy spectacle rekindled all my hatred of Catholicism. I passed through the Ghetto, and as I beheld the misery and degradation of the Jews, I said to myself that it was a loftier thing to be on the side of the oppressed than on that of the oppressors."

Our conversation now took a controversial turn; I tried, in my eager fervor, to impart to him my own Catholic convictions. But he only smiled at my efforts, saying that he felt a sincere pity for my superstition, and that he was born a Jew and a Jew he would die.

Now there came into my head an extraordinary idea, one the wise of this world would call foolish.

"Since you are so confident," I said, "in the strength and stability of your understanding, promise to wear something I will give you."

"Let me see it first," he replied. "What sort of thing is it?"

"Only this medal," said I, and I held up to him a medal of the Blessed Virgin, at the sight of which he threw himself back in his chair with a gesture of indignation and astonishment.

"But," said I, quietly, "from your point of view it must be a matter of perfect indifference, whereas it would give me the very greatest pleasure."

"Oh, I will not refuse you," he exclaimed with a hearty laugh. "I shall at least show you that people have no right to accuse us Jews of obstinate and insurmountable prejudice. Besides, you are furnishing me with a charming chapter for my notes and impressions of my travels." And he went on with a series of jests which wrung my heart, for to me they were so many blasphemies.

However, I threw around his neck the ribbon to which one of my daughters had attached the medal while we were talking. There remained a more difficult point to gain. I wished him to recite St. Bernard's prayer, *Memorare, o piissima Virgo*. This was too much for him. He refused most decidedly, and in a tone that seemed to say, *Really, this man's impertinence is beyond all bounds*. Still I combated his repeated refusals with the energy of desperation. I held out the prayer to him and begged him to take it with him, and asked him also to be kind enough to write out a copy for me, as I did not possess another.

At length he yielded, as if to rid himself of my importunity.

"Well, I will write it out for you," he said in a tone of vexation and contempt. "You shall have my copy and I will keep yours."

After he was gone, my wife and I looked at each other for some time without speaking a word. Distressed by the blasphemy we had heard, we united in imploring pardon from God for him, and we charged our two little daughters to say a Hail Mary at night for his conversion.

From this point every circumstance seems so important to a clear account of this great work of God, that I feel it a duty to relate everything that passed, from the day when Ratisbonne carried away the Memorare to the moment when the Mother of Mercy removed the veil which obstructed his soul's vision, and he received the grace to make a public profession of the Catholic faith.

At first Ratisbonne could not get over his astonishment at my importunity. He copied out the prayer, however, and read it again and again, in order to discover what could give it such worth in my estimation, and why I ascribed to it such a mighty efficacy. Eventually he had learned it by heart. It recurred to his memory continually, and he went about repeating it mechanically, just as we unconsciously hum a tune which has struck our fancy.

For my part, I felt entirely absorbed in the result of my conversation with a man of whom I knew next to nothing, and with whom I had spoken that day for the first time. I could not account for the internal force that impelled me towards him, and inspired me with a deep, inexplicable conviction that sooner or later God would open his eyes.

I resolved to prevent, at all costs, his departure from Rome. I went that evening to visit him at the Hotel Serny and, as he was not there, left a note for him, asking him to call on me the following day, Sunday, at half past ten in the morning.

On Saturday evening it was my turn to watch before the Blessed Sacrament, according to the pious custom at Rome, in company with Prince M.A.B. and some other friends. I begged them to join me in my prayers to obtain of God the conversion of a Jew.

The next morning, Ratisbonne came punctually at the appointed hour, and said to me in an offhand way, "Well, I hope you have forgotten your dreams of yesterday. I have come to say good bye to you; I am off tonight."

"My dreams!" I replied. "The thoughts you are pleased to call dreams occupy me more than ever; and as to your going away, we will not speak of that, for you absolutely must put it off for a week."

"Oh, that is impossible. I have reserved my place."

"What does that matter? We will go together to the office to say that you have changed your mind and are not going."

"Now, this is going too far. Most decidedly, I leave tonight."

"Most decidedly, you will not leave tonight, even if I have to lock you up in my own room."

And I told him that he could not leave Rome without having seen some grand ceremony at St. Peter's, and that in a very few days he would have an excellent opportunity to do so. He was so amazed at my pertinacity that he allowed me to lead him off to the office to erase his name from the list of travelers. Then we visited the houses of the Augustinians and the Jesuits.

I dined that same day at the Borghese palace, in company with the Count de Laferronnays. During the evening I told him of my hopes, and earnestly commended my young Jewish friend to his prayers. De Laferronnays spoke to me of the confidence he had always felt in the protection of the Blessed Virgin, even during the time when the cares and distractions of political life had permitted little of that practical piety of which his later life was so edifying an example.

"Keep up a good hope," said he. "If he says the Memorare, you have him to a certainty, and many others with him."

On Monday afternoon, I walked about Rome with Ratisbonne. I was grieved to notice the little fruit of our conversations. He was still in the same frame of mind—still hated Catholicism intensely, and made the most disparaging remarks about it—still parried with raillery arguments he thought not worth the trouble of serious refutation.

De Laferronnays died that night. In the afternoon he accompanied my children, his daughter and his son-in-law, the Count de Meun, to St. John Lateran. There he prayed a long time before the Blessed Sacrament, as was his custom. He complained a little of a pain in the chest, which came on at intervals, and was so sharp and sudden that it prevented his walking; but in all other respects he was as cheerful and lively as usual. My children met him again at Benediction, in the chapel of perpetual adoration, on the Quirinal.

There was a brilliant reception that evening at the Austrian embassy. Madame de Laferronnays was to take her daughters there, and while they were dressing their father amused himself by playing with his grandchild. It was between half-past eight and nine. He complained still of his pain, but as it was habitual, his family were sorry for it, but felt no serious anxiety. They attributed it to the effects of a brazier they had put into his room to warm it, the heat of which had drawn the blood to his chest. Still, they sent for his physician.

Madame de Laferronnays also wrote to the Abbe Gerbet, but was not so alarmed as to send the letter immediately. When the physician arrived, he advised bleeding, and a surgeon was sent for. But the pain became easier; they thought the crisis past, and stopped the bleeding. Then the return of the pain made them send again for the surgeon, who made two fruitless attempts to bleed him. He now suffered acutely, and cries of anguish escaped him in spite of himself.

His wife was in keen distress, walking about and trying to avoid hearing his moans, when a few brief words told her the imminence of the danger. She sat down upon his bed and took his hand, and did not leave him again. She sat in perfect calm, full of gentleness and resignation. The Abbe Gerbet arrived and gave him absolution. Then his face regained its usual serenity, and showed the calm of his soul.

"How happy I feel now!" he said, in a failing voice, but with a smile of confidence and hope. But soon his breathing became more difficult.

"Adieu," he said to his beloved wife. "Adieu, my dear children," and so, in a few moments, his soul appeared before God, while his young daughters knelt beside his bed in their festive dresses. It was only half past ten.

I have before me a letter he wrote less than a year before his death.

I leave Rome with regret, and but for the important matters which summon me to France, I should certainly have prolonged my stay. For him who is blessed with faith, for him who has ever held lonely conversation with himself in that city of silence and of faith, Rome is the city to live and to die in. I admire as much as anyone else the colossal ruins that give one so grand an idea of what ancient Rome must have been, and the wonderful people who raised them. I can well understand why the imagination should be enthralled among these stately relics; yet it is not the ruins that fascinate me, or the recollection of ancient time that makes me sorry to leave the city. It is the soil of those theaters moistened with the blood of thousands of martyrs, the precious remains of those heroes of the Faith, here preserved and venerated on the very spot of their glorious agony. It is the sacred dust of the catacombs, the hallowed ground that has witnessed the sufferings and the triumphs of the Church; it is the unshakable rock, against which the impotent efforts of impiety, heresy and philosophism have been broken and thrown back, age after age—this throne of the poor fisherman, set up on the ruins of the throne of the Caesars.

 O my friend, how can one see all this, and not believe? How can one help feeling at Rome some presentiment of our eternal destiny? How can we miss seeing whence our souls came, and whither they are going? How can people come to Rome to see only lifeless stones? To a Catholic soul Rome is Catholic Rome. It is the land of Catholic memorials, of Catholic miracles, of Catholic hopes. Here one's faith grows stronger; here the Catholic raises a corner of the veil which shrouds the sublime mysteries of our religion. Here the heart of the Catholic sees with a clear and distinct intuition the vanity and nothingness of the pomps and glories of this world, and already breathes the calm and genial atmosphere of eternity.

My days here are all too short. May God grant that I may once again see Rome. Yes, it is at Rome that I would live and die.

And God heard his prayer.

His death occasioned much grief. He left to his sorrowing family and friends the memory of an edifying example, and the consoling hope that God had called him because he was ripe for Heaven. He was so affectionate and so gentle, that he was loved by everyone. His body lay in state three days in the Palazzo Spina. Having long loved him as my own father, I had my part not only in the sorrow of his family, but also in the mournful duties which fell upon them. Still, the thought of Ratisbonne followed me importunately even beside the bier of my friend.

I passed part of Monday night with the family of de Laferronnays, and felt unwilling to leave them, but I could not banish from my mind this soul whom I was so anxious to subdue to the Faith. I told the Abbe Gerbet of my conflict. He had been for many years de Laferronnays' chaplain and friend.

"Go," said he. "Carry on the work you have begun. In doing so you will best fulfill the wishes of our deceased friend, who prayed fervently for the conversion of this young man."

So early on Tuesday I went and found Ratisbonne, and took possession of him. I brought him to various religious antiquities, in order to keep the great truths of Catholicism in his mind. I got him to visit the Church of

Aracoeli again. If he felt any return of his emotion it was very temporarily, for he listened coldly to me, and answered all my observations with witticisms.

"I will turn these things over in my mind when I am at Malta," he said. "I shall have plenty of time on my hands, for I am to spend two months there, and I shall be glad of anything to keep me from boredom."

On Wednesday Ratisbonne and I walked in the direction of the Capitol and Forum. Close by, on the Coelian Hill, is the Church of St. Stefano Rotundo, the walls of which are covered with frescoes that represent with terrible fidelity the various torments of the early martyrs. Ratisbonne was horrified as we looked at them.

"It is a hideous sight," said he, as though to anticipate my observations, "but those of your religion were quite as cruel to the poor Jews in the middle ages as the persecutors of antiquity were to the Christians."

But at St. John Lateran I showed him the bas reliefs above the statues of the apostles. On one side are the figures of the Old Testament, on the other their fulfillment in the person of the Messiah. The comparison seemed to him ingenious.

We continued toward the Villa Wolkonski. Ratisbonne said he was surprised at my calm; he could not reconcile it with my eager desire for his conversion, and he remarked that he was more than ever a Jew. I answered that I was full of confidence in the promises of God, and that I was convinced that, since he was honest and sincere, he would one day be a Catholic, even if an angel from Heaven were necessary to enlighten him.

We were than passing by the Holy Steps. I took off my hat and, pointing to my companion, said, "Hail! Scala

Santa, here is a man who will one day ascend you on his knees."

Ratisbonne burst into a fit of laughter, and we separated without my being able to indulge the feeblest hope that I had, in any degree, shaken his convictions. But I believed Him who said, *Knock, and it shall be opened to you.* I returned to pray beside the remains of my beloved friend; and as I knelt I asked him to aid in the conversion of my young friend, if, as I hoped, he had already attained the rest of the blessed.

Around noon on Thursday, Ratisbonne went into a café on the Piazza di Spagna to read the newspapers. There he found my brother-in-law, Edmund Humann; they chatted over the news of the day with a flippancy and an ease which excluded all idea of any serious preoccupation of mind. At about half past twelve, as he came out of the café, he met his friend the Baron de Lotzbeck, and conversed with him on the most frivolous matters. They spoke of dancing, of pleasure and of the reception given by the Duke de Torlonia.

At one o'clock I had to make some arrangements at the Church of San Andrea delle Fratte for the funeral the next day. Ratisbonne met me in the Via Condotti. He would go with me to the church and wait for me a few minutes; then we would go for our walk.

When we entered the church, Ratisbonne noticed the preparations for the funeral, and asked for whom they were made.

"For a friend I have just lost," said I, "and whom I loved very much, de Laferronnays."

He then began to walk around the nave, and his cold, indifferent look seemed to say, *This is certainly a very ugly church.* I left him on the epistle side, to the right of a small enclosure destined to receive the coffin, and went into the convent. I wanted a gallery prepared for the family of the deceased, so they would not have to observe the funeral from outside the enclosure; my absence could not have been more than ten or twelve minutes.

When I came back into the church I saw nothing of Ratisbonne for a moment; then I caught sight of him on his knees, in front of the chapel of St. Michael the Archangel. I went up to him, and touched him three or four times before he became aware of my presence. Finally he turned to me, tears on his face. He joined his hands together and said, "How this gentleman has prayed for me!"

I was thoroughly astonished. I raised Ratisbonne and led him, or rather almost carried him, out of the church. I asked him what was the matter, and where he wished to go.

"Lead me where you please," he replied. "After what I have seen, I obey."

I urged him to explain his meaning, but he could not. He drew out his miraculous medal, however, and kissed it.

I brought him to his apartment, but notwithstanding my repeated questions, I could get nothing from him but such exclamations as: "How good is the Lord! What a fullness of grace and happiness! How pitiable the lot of those who know it not!"

And he wept at the thought of heretics and unbelievers. At length he asked if I did not think him mad.

"But no," he said, "I am in my senses. My God, I am not beside myself. Everyone knows I am not mad."

Ratisbonne gradually became more calm, and then he embraced me. His face was radiant—I might almost say transfigured. He begged me to take him to a confessor. He wanted to know when he could receive Baptism, for he could not live without it. He yearned for the blessedness of the martyrs whose sufferings he had seen depicted on the walls of San Stefano Rotundo. He told me that he could give me no explanation of his state until he had received permission from a priest to do so.

"What I have to say," he added, "is something I can say only on my knees."

I took him to the Gesu to see Fr. de Villefort, who asked him to explain himself. Then Ratisbonne drew forth his medal, kissed it, showed it to us and exclaimed, "I have seen her!"

Soon he regained his calmness, and made his statement.

"I had been in the church only a few moments," he said, "when I was suddenly seized with a profound agitation of mind. The building disappeared from before me. One single chapel had, so to speak, gathered and concentrated all the light. In the midst of the radiance I saw standing on the altar, tall, clothed in splendor, full of majesty and sweetness, the Virgin Mary, just as she appears on my medal. An irresistible force drew me towards her. She made a sign with her hand that I should kneel; and then she seemed to say, 'That will do.' She spoke not a work, but I understood all."

We listened to him with awe, marveling at the depth of the counsels of God, and at His mercy. One phrase especially struck us: "She spoke not a word, but I understood all."

Indeed, the Catholic faith breathed from him. He spoke of the Real Presence like a man who believed it with all the energy of his being; but that expression is too weak— he spoke like one to whom it was an object of direct perception.

On leaving Fr. de Villefort, we went to give thanks to God, first at Santa Maria Maggiore, the favored basilica of the Blessed Virgin, and then at St. Peter's.

"Now I understand," Ratisbonne said to me, "the love with which Catholics regard their churches, and the piety which leads them to adorn them. How good it is to be here! One longs never to leave. It is earth no longer; it is the vestibule of Heaven."

At the altar of the Blessed Sacrament, the Real Presence so overwhelmed him that I was obliged to lead him away, so awful did it seem to him to appear before the living God with the stain of original sin upon him. He took refuge in the chapel of the Blessed Virgin.

"Here," he said, "I can have no fear. I feel myself under the protection of an unlimited mercy."

He prayed with great fervor at the tombs of the apostles. The story of St. Paul's conversion, which I related to him, much impressed him.

He was astonished at the strength of the posthumous bond—his words—that united him to de Laferronnays. He wished to pass the night beside his remains. Gratitude, he said, made it a duty. But Fr. de Villefort, seeing that he was exhausted, prudently opposed this pious wish, and advised him not to remain later than ten o'clock.

Ratisbonne then told us that the night before he had not been able to sleep much. He had had always before his eyes a large cross, of peculiar form, and without the image of the Lord.

"I made," he said, "incredible efforts to drive away this figure, but they were all fruitless." Some hours later, his eye casually fell upon the reverse of his medal, and he recognized his cross as the one he had seen.

Meanwhile I was impatient to return to the family of de Laferronnays. I had consolation to give them, at the moment when his remains were about to be taken from them.

I entered the chamber of death in a state of agitation, I might almost say of joy, which at once attracted the attention of all present, and showed them I had something of importance to communicate. They all followed me into an adjoining room, and I hastily told all that had occurred.

I had brought them tidings from Heaven. Their tears of grief were in a moment changed into tears of gratitude. Their poor hearts could now bear with perfect resignation that keenest of sacrifices—the last farewell to the remains of him they had loved.

Then I was eager to see again the son whom God had just given me. He had begged me not to leave him—had needed, he said, a friend to whom he could tell the experiences of such a day.

I asked him about the circumstances of the miraculous vision. He was quite unable to explain how he had passed from the right side of the church to the chapel, which is on the left, and from which he was separated by the preparations that had been made for the funeral. All he knew was that he had found himself suddenly on his knees, and then prostrate, close to this chapel. At first he had been able to see clearly the Queen of Heaven in all the splendor of her beauty; but he could not long bear that radiance. Thrice he had tried to gaze once more upon the Mother of Mercy; thrice he proved his inability to raise his eyes beyond her hands.

"O my God!" he cried. "I who only a half hour before was still blaspheming! I who felt such a deadly hatred of the Catholic religion! And all who know me know well enough that, humanly speaking, I have the strongest reasons for remaining a Jew. My family is Jewish; my bride is Jewish; my uncle is a Jew. In becoming a Catholic, I sacrifice all the interests and all the hopes I have on earth; and yet I am not mad. Everyone knows that I am not mad, that I have never been mad. Surely they must receive my testimony."

On Friday the news of the miracle began to spread through Rome. With customary caution, people were on guard lest they should receive a statement so startling on insufficient testimony. But doubt soon became impossible in the presence of the facts. Everyone seemed to bless God for the privilege of being in Rome at a time when it had pleased Him to quicken our confidence in the Immaculate Virgin, by attesting in so wonderful a way to the power of her intercession. Everyone wanted to see the happy young man for whom the Mother of Divine Grace had descended from Heaven.

I was with Ratisbonne at Fr. de Villefort's, when General Chlapouski was announced. "Sir," said he, "so you have seen the likeness of the Blessed Virgin. Tell me all about it."

"The likeness, sir!" cried Ratisbonne. "The likeness! I have seen her herself, in reality, in her own person, just as I see you there before me."

Even if we can imagine an illusion in the case of a person of Ratisbonne's character and education, with prejudices so violent, and with such interest both of affection and of position, it could not have been induced or augmented by any outward representation; for in the chapel that was the scene of the miracle, there is no statue, or picture, or image of the Blessed Virgin of any kind.

I was anxious that Ratisbonne should be introduced to the family of de Laferronnays. It seemed right that he should alleviate their sorrow by telling them of the tie of everlasting gratitude by which it had pleased God to link his soul to the one that had just left them. He was too much affected to talk consecutively. He could do little more than press the hands held out to him, as to a beloved child.

"Oh, believe my words," he said to them. "It is to the prayers of M. de Laferronnays that I owe my conversion."

The new convert spent at my house the few days that passed before the retreat in which he was to prepare for his baptism. He read me some parts of his letters to his bride, to his uncle, to all the members of his family. In our conversations he often returned to the obvious proofs, which ought to convince the most skeptical, of the miraculous intervention that effected his conversion.

"The weightiest inducements," he said, "the strongest interests, bound me to my religion. A man has a claim to be believed, when he sacrifices everything to a conviction which must have come from Heaven. If all that I have said is not rigorously true, I commit a crime, not only the most daring, but the most senseless and motiveless. In making my entrance into Catholicism by a sacrilegious lie, I not only risk my position in this world, but I lose my soul, and assume the frightful responsibility of all those whom my example may induce to do as I am doing. And what interest can I have in this?

"Alas, when my brother became a Catholic, and a priest, I persecuted him with a more unrelenting fury than any other member of my family. We were completely sundered. I hated him with a virulent hatred, although he had fully pardoned me. I trust that God may send me the severest of tests, that His own glory may be advanced, and that the world may know that I am sincere."

And surely we cannot question the sincerity and good faith of a man who, in his twenty-eighth year, sacrifices all the joys of his heart, all the hopes of his life, at the call of conscience. He knew well all the consequences of his resolution; he knew that Christianity is the worship of the Cross; again and again he was told of the trials that awaited him, and of the duties laid upon him by the religion he was so eager to embrace.

From the moment in which he requested the sacrament of Baptism, he was placed under the care of the venerable father who rules a society justly dear to every Christian. This good father, after hearing his story with his usual kindness, and at the same time with calm gravity, urged him to weigh well the sacrifices he would be compelled to make, the serious obligations he would have to fulfill, the peculiar conflicts which awaited him, the temptations and trials to which a step like his would expose him; and then, pointing to a crucifix which stood on the table, he said:

"That cross you saw in your sleep, when once you have been baptized, you must not only worship it, but bear it." And then, opening the Scriptures, he turned to the second chapter of Ecclesiasticus and read to Ratisbonne these words:

> "Son, when thou comest to the service of God, stand in justice and in fear, and prepare thy soul for temptation. Humble thy heart and endure: incline thine ear, and receive the words of understanding: and make not haste in the time of clouds. Wait on God with patience; join thyself to God, and endure, that thy life may be increased in the latter end. Take all that shall be brought upon thee and in thy sorrow endure, and in

thy humiliation keep patience. For gold and silver are tried in the fire, but acceptable men in the furnace of humiliation. Believe God, and He will recover thee: and direct thy way; and trust in Him. Keep His fear, and grow old therein."

These words produced a deep impression on Ratisbonne. They strengthened his resolution, and gave him very serious and sober ideas about Christianity. He listened in silence, but at the close of the retreat that preceded his baptism, he went in the evening to see the holy priest who had read him those words a week before, and begged for a copy of them, that he might preserve them, and meditate on them every day of his life.

Such are the facts which I submit to the consideration of all thoughtful men, for the edification of those who believe and for the instruction of those who are still seeking. I shall think myself happy if, having wandered too long in the gloom and contradictions of the Protestant sects, I may by this narrative excite in some erring brother the will to cry, *Lord, that my eyes may be opened!* For everyone who truly prays will soon have his eyes opened to the sunlight of Catholic truth.

Those who gained admission to the church of the Jesuits on January 31 will not readily forget the ceremony which publicly authenticated one of those marvels of grace by which God would revive the faith of the lukewarm, and lead into the right way those who are now walking in darkness.

Long before the appointed hour the Church of the Gesu, which had been chosen by the Cardinal Vicar, was filled by a crowd eager to see this young Jew whom the Virgin herself has deigned to bring to the foot of the Cross. There were present many wandering sheep, curious persons who long to see anything novel or striking; but a contagious reverence pervaded the congregation.

Prudent precautions had been taken to preserve the order that was necessary for the edification of all. The space between the altar of St. Ignatius and that of St. Francis Xavier was prepared for the accommodation of the large crowd, and the zeal of true Christians had forestalled the eagerness of the merely curious, and thrown around the altar the protection of their reverent silence and devout prayers.

At about half past eight Ratisbonne, wearing the white robe of a catechumen, was led in by Fr. de Villefort and Baron de Bussieres, his sponsor, and took his place in the chapel of St. Andrew, near the principal entrance of the church. During the half-hour that followed, he was naturally the object of general curiosity, but he endured this test with great resignation.

At nine o'clock Cardinal Patrizi, vicar of the Pope, began to offer the prayers for the baptism of adults, psalms that seem as though they had been written expressly to clothe in words the feelings of the catechumen, and to describe how the Lord had been pleased to call him to the truth. *Spera in Deo, quoniam adhuc confitebor illi: salutare vultus mei, et Deus meus.* Hope in God, for I will still give praise to Him: the salvation of my countenance and my God. *Introibo ad altare Dei.* I will go unto the altar of God.

Then His Eminence proceeded to the lower end of the church. There Fr. de Villefort and Baron de Bussieres presented the young Jew to him.

"What do you ask of the Church of God?"

"Faith."

The Conversion of Ratisbonne

And this faith, this holy Catholic faith, was his already. The bright morning star had already risen upon him, and enlightened him with its clear shining. When commanded to "put away with contempt the superstition of the Hebrews," he hesitated not a moment, and the firmness of his replies showed him worthy of the favor the Church had granted him, in abridging the usual tests for catechumens.

The Cardinal breathed thrice upon him, to put to flight the spirit of evil; he marked him with the sign of the Cross, and gave him to taste the salt of wisdom, and said over him the prayers of exorcism.

But there was one last, unexpected, test.

"Kiss the dust."

Calmly, unhesitatingly, he obeyed. No doubt remained that he was a Christian indeed, for he had intuitively discovered that humility is the strait gate that leads to truth and salvation. Eloquent lesson for us all, who are too prone to forget that our Master was meek and lowly in heart!

There could be no doubt. The mind that was in Christ was in this candidate for Christ's service. The Church hesitated no longer. She remembered no more his life in times past, or his blasphemies of yesterday. She sees him only as the privileged child of Mary. The Cardinal placed the end of his stole in Ratisbonne's hand, in token of his adoption, and to teach him that in the Catholic family the children must lean trustfully on their fathers. In triumph he led this beloved sheep of the fold to the altar of St. Ignatius.

How shall I describe the reaction of the congregation as Ratisbonne passed? His face was a blend of decision and gentleness; his measured step, his white garment carried them in thought back to the Church of the catacombs.

Some worthy Roman women expressed in their own

simple way the charity that all the observers felt. "*Ah, quanto sei caro! Ah, beato lui!*" And then they kissed their rosaries, and pointed with affectionate curiosity to de Bussieres: "See, he is a Frenchman—it was he who gave the medal to the Jew, who made him pray to the Blessed Virgin. *Ma che buon signore! Che Dio le benedica!*"

Then the Cardinal was standing near the altar, and Ratisbonne knelt before him to receive Baptism.

"What is your name?"

"Marie," is his reply, with gratitude and love, the name of the Queen of Patriarchs, who has opened to him the gates of the Church.

"Do you renounce the Devil?"

"I renounce him."

"And all his pomps?"

"I renounce them."

"And all his works?"

"I renounce them."

"Do you believe in God, the Father Almighty, Creator of Heaven and earth?

"I believe in Him."

"Do you believe in Jesus Christ, His only Son, our Lord, who was born and suffered for us?

"I believe in Him."

"Do you believe in the Holy Ghost, the Holy Catholic Church, the Communion of Saints, the remission of sins, the resurrection of the flesh and the life everlasting?"

"I do believe."

"And now, what do you desire?

"Baptism."

At length Marie Alphonse Ratisbonne rises up a Christian—a Christian pure and fervent as the angels who stand about the throne of God. He holds in his hand the blessed taper whose flame signifies the light of submissive faith which neither wavers nor misleads. The laying on of hands and the unction with holy chrism impart to him a second grace, in confirming the fullness of what he has already received. Henceforward Ratisbonne is a disciple of the Cross, prepared to confess the Faith to all.

Then Abbot Dupanloup, soon to be Bishop of Orleans, addressed to the congregation some words about the goodness of our God.

"The providence of God is wondrous in all its designs and in all its methods, and deeply are they to be pitied who can neither comprehend nor extol it. For them the life of man is but a mournful mystery, his days a chain whose links are twined by fate and man himself but a creature, noble indeed, but accursed in every faculty, utterly forgotten by a God who heeds neither his virtues nor his sorrows.

"But Thou, O my God, art not thus unheeding, neither hast Thou thus fashioned us. Notwithstanding our profound misery, Thy providence still keeps watch over us. Higher than highest mountains, deeper far and wider than the great and wide sea, it is an abyss unfathomable of power, and wisdom, and of love. I bless Thee above all, I adore Thee, because from Thy lofty and eternal dwelling-place Thou dost remember, and remember with compassion, the creatures Thy hand hath formed—because from the Heavens Thou dost bestow a look of pity and of love on us—because, as the Prophet says, Thou dost shake the Heavens and the earth, and multiply Thy prodigies, in order to save those whom Thou lovest, in order to save just one soul.

"And you, on whom every eye is now turned, who are you? What is your petition in this holy place? What homage do you come to pay? What means that robe of stainless white you wear? What power has so suddenly changed your purposes?

"Tell us how, like Abraham, your great ancestor—Abraham, whose true son you have this day become—you were going on, following the voice of the Lord, but not knowing whither you went, your eyes sealed in darkness until you reached the holy city. Tell us, why do you thus enter into our possession, as into your own heritage? Yesterday you were but a stranger and a sojourner with us. Who has placed you thus at home in our midst?

"Hail Mary, full of grace! Thou lovest to shower down on us the plenitude of thy mother's heart. The Lord is with thee! It is through thee that He has been pleased to come down among us. I must range the courts of Heaven in quest of images to set forth thy dignity and thy praise. Thy name is sweeter to us than earth's purest joy, more helpful and gentle to the guilty heart, when it repents, that is the dew of evening to the leaves which the scorching heat of noon has withered. It is thou who settest again in the right way the feet of the wandering traveler, and thou dost herald the rising of the Sun of justice in our hearts.

"At thy name, O Mary, the Heavens rejoice, and earth sings for gladness of heart, while Hell shudders in impotent wrath. None can truly invoke thine aid and perish. I have seen the wildest spots of earth smile at thy name and put on gracefulness; pious dwellers in far-off wildernesses sing thy glories.

"O God, open the eyes of those who see not, that they may see Mary, and know the sweet radiance of her mother's eyes. Touch the hearts which love her not.

"Brother well beloved—and I am happy in being the

first to greet you by this name—you see under what favorable auspices you make your entry into the new Jerusalem, the dwelling-place of God, into the Church of the living God, which is the pillar and ground of the truth.

"I dare not hide from you its most austere teaching. You have understood all, you tell us. But permit me to ask you, have you understood the mystery of the cross? Take good heed—it is the basis and groundwork of Christianity.

"I do not mean now that hallowed Cross which you revere because it brings to your mind Christ crucified in expiation for your sins. Let me borrow the energetic language of an ancient apologist of our faith, and say to you: We are not now concerned with the Cross which it is so blessed to revere, but with that cross which you must learn to bear. It can scarcely be that your future life should offer you no crosses to be borne. I see them preparing. I am greatly deceived if patience be not the appointed means of increasing and strengthening your faith, and enabling you to bring forth its fruits.

"You have been brought within the Christian Church by Mary and by the Cross. Son of the Catholic Church, you will share the destiny of your mother. Look out on Rome. Continuous conflict and continuous triumph—this is her earthly heritage.

"It is today your Pentecost, and the Spirit of might and of love has filled your heart. It is today your Paschaltime, and Jesus Christ is about to feed you with His Body and Blood. Jesus Christ is far too truly our God and our friend to feed our souls with an empty image; besides, He commands us to love Him so as to be ready to lay down our lives for Him, and the Eucharist has always been the food and the strength of martyrs.

"Abraham, Isaac and Jacob, patriarchs and prophets cheer you on from Heaven; and Moses gives you his blessing, because the law written in your heart has recognized the Gospel; and it is Mary who receives and protects you.

"O Mary, it is an imperious wish of our hearts, no less than a duty, to offer once again the prayer to which we owe, it may be, this happy day. Remember, O most gracious Virgin Mary, that never was it known that anyone who fled to thy protection, implored thine aid and sought thine intercession and was left unanswered. Inspired by this confidence, we turn to thee, O Virgin of Virgins. To thee we come, before thee we stand, sinful and sorrowful. O Mother of the Word Incarnate, remember now those who stand in grace, and those who are in sin. I will not say, Remember this youth, for he is thy child. But remember the friends for whom he offers this day his first Catholic prayers. Restore them to him in time, restore them to him in eternity.

"And since I am also a stranger here—but no, there are no strangers at Rome, since every Catholic is a Roman—since we were both born on the soil of France, I say, Remember France; it has still noble virtues, generous souls. Bring back upon the Church in France the fair beauty of the days of old."

The holy sacrifice of the Mass closed the ceremony. Especially at the solemn moment of Communion Our Lord seemed to pour His grace upon the solemn congregation. Our brother Ratisbonne was so overcome by his consciousness of the Divine Presence that it was necessary to support him as he drew near the holy table, and after having received the Bread of angels he was unable to rise without the aid of Fr. de Villefort and his sponsor. And the profound exclamation of the convert was in all our thoughts: "I understood all."

After the Te Deum, the Cardinal led the new child of the Church into the house of the Jesuits. He wished to spend in retreat the days of carnival which were drawing near.

But there remained one duty to be discharged. He longed for the moment when he might cast himself at the feet of the venerable Pontiff who guides with so sure a hand the bark which bears us all towards our eternal haven. Ratisbonne and de Bussieres were introduced to the Pope by the general of the Company of Jesus, and received the mighty benediction which Catholics prize so highly.

The Holy Father conversed with them for some time, and gave them many tokens of his affection, with all the frank and tender love of a father. He gave directions that they should be taken to see the interior of his palace. Pushing them before him with gracious familiarity, he brought them into his bedroom. Then the successor of the prince of the apostles gave them evidence of his own trust in the protection of Mary, Help of Christians. He showed them an image of the Blessed Virgin which he reveres with a special devotion, and which is placed close to his bed. And then, wishing that Ratisbonne should preserve some memorial of his visit, His Holiness gave him a crucifix to which special indulgences were attached.

And if, when days of trial and conflict come, the new soldier should need to refresh his courage, let him behold that crucifix and say confidently, *In hoc signo vinces*. Every young life is exposed to storm; happier than we are, he has been crowned before the conflict, but the evil days will come. May he then remember his brethren at Rome! May he never forget Mary, his mother!

The Narrative of Marie-Alphonse Ratisbonne

My family is known well enough, for its members are rich and generous, and it has long occupied a high station in Alsace. It is said that my ancestors were very godly men; Christians as well as Jews have blessed the name of my grandfather, the only Jew who obtained, under Louis XVI, not only the right to hold property at Strasbourg, but a patent of nobility. Such was my family; but now all traditions of religion are effaced from it.

I began my studies at the Royal College of Strasbourg, where I made far greater progress in the depravation of my heart than in the education of my mind.

In the year 1825 (I was born in 1814), an unexpected event inflicted a heavy blow upon my family. My brother Theodore, of whom the highest hopes were entertained, avowed himself a Christian. Soon after, in spite of the grief he had caused and the earnest entreaties of our parents, he became a priest, and exercised his ministry in the same city—before the very eyes of my disconsolate family.

Young as I was, my brother's conduct shocked me greatly, and I conceived a violent hatred of his office, and of his person. Brought up among young Christians who were quite as reckless and indifferent as I was myself, I had not up until that time felt either sympathy or antipathy towards Christianity; but my brother's conversion, which I regarded as an act of unaccountable folly, made me believe all I heard of the fanaticism of the Catholics, and I held them now in great horror.

The Conversion of Ratisbonne

I was at about that time withdrawn from my college to be placed in a Protestant institution, the prospectus of which had dazzled my parents. The younger members of the great Protestant families of Alsace and Germany came there, to be molded upon the fashionable life of Paris, and abandoned themselves to pleasures of all kinds, far more than to study. Nevertheless, I presented myself for examination when I left there and, by a piece of good luck I little deserved, I graduated Bachelor of Arts.

I was then the sole master of my patrimony, for my mother had died while I was still young, and my father had survived her only a few years. But I had a worthy uncle, the patriarch of the family, a second father to me who, having no children of his own, gave all his affection to those of his brother.

This uncle, so well known in the financial world for his lofty integrity as well as for his extraordinary abilities, wished very much to give me a share in the bank of which he is the head. First, however, I studied law in Paris.

Having obtained my diploma, I was recalled to Strasbourg by my uncle, who exerted all his influence to settle me with him. I cannot count all his cares and kindnesses—horses, carriages, pleasant travels, a thousand acts of lavish affection. He had not the heart to refuse me anything. He gave me the signature of the bank, and promised me also the title and the solid advantages of a partner—a promise he carried into effect the first day of this year, 1842. I was at Rome when this information reached me.

My uncle had only one complaint—my frequent journeys to Paris. "You are too fond of the Champs-Elysees," said he affectionately.

He was right. I loved nothing but pleasure. Business annoyed me, the atmosphere of the office stifled me. I had a notion that people came into the world simply to enjoy themselves and, while a kind of natural and instinctive modesty kept me from baser pleasures and associates, I thought of nothing but receptions and parties, and gave myself up to them with passion.

It was fortunate that about this time a good work offered itself to my eager need of action, and I threw myself into it with all my heart. It was the work of the regeneration of the poor Israelites. I became one of the most zealous members of a society that provided occupations for young Jews. I managed to fill its coffers, and fancied I had done something very great.

Although I had no religion at all, I was busy with the worldly condition of my coreligionists. I was a Jew by profession, and that was all, for I did not even believe in God. I never opened a religious book, and neither in my uncle's house nor in those of my brothers and sisters was there the slightest observance of the injunctions of Judaism.

I was not happy, although I possessed everything in abundance, in profusion. Something was still lacking; and this something I found.

I had a niece, the daughter of my eldest brother, who had been intended for me from our childhood. She was growing up before my eyes in beauty and gracefulness, and in her I saw the fair promise of my future life and the satisfaction of all my hopes. Those who have seen her know that it would not be easy to imagine a young girl more gentle, more amiable, more charming. She was to me a creature apart, who seemed meant to complete my existence. When the desires of all our family, combined with our mutual sympathy and affection, fixed the time of my marriage, I thought that nothing could be wanting to my happiness.

After the ceremony of our betrothal, I had the pleasure of seeing all my family filled with joy, and my sisters especially happy. They had only one reproach to make—I loved my future wife too exclusively, and they confessed their jealousy. There are few families so happy as mine: the affection that reigns among my brothers and sisters verges on idolatry; and my sisters are so good, so loving and so lovely.

There was only one member of my family who was hateful to me—my brother Theodore, although he loved us well. His soutane repelled me, his presence oppressed me with gloom, his grave and serious conversation excited my wrath. About a year before my betrothal I had found it impossible to restrain my feelings, and I expressed them to him in a letter which was intended to sever all connections between us forever.

The occasion was this. A child was lying in the agony of death; my brother Theodore had the audacity to ask permission to baptize him. He probably would have succeeded if I had not been informed of his intention. I looked on it as an unworthy and dishonorable attempt. I wrote to the *priest* to try his strength with men and not with children, and accompanied these words with such invective that I am even now astonished that my brother did not answer me a single word. I would never see him again, and I cherished a bitter hatred against priests, churches and convents, and especially against the Jesuits, whose very name goaded me to frenzy.

Fortunately my brother left Strasbourg, and so gratified my most earnest wish. He was summoned to Paris, to Notre Dame des Victoires where, he said as he bade us farewell, he should not cease to pray for the conversion of his brothers and sisters. His departure relieved me of a heavy weight. I even yielded so far to the entreaties of my family as to write him a few words of apology on the occasion of my betrothal. He answered my letter affectionately, and commended to my care some poor people in whom he felt interested; and I gave them some trifling sum.

After this sort of reconciliation I had no further connection with Theodore, and I had altogether ceased to think of him.

A change did take place in my religious notions about the time of the ceremony of my betrothal. As I have said, I believed in nothing; and in this complete nullity, this negation of all faith, I found myself perfectly in harmony with my young friends, whether Catholic or Protestant. But the look of my future bride awakened within me a mysterious sense of human dignity and worth. I began to believe in the immortality of the soul. More than that, I began, by a kind of instinct, to pray to God. I thanked him for my happiness, although I was not happy. I could not account for my feelings.

It was thought right, because of the youth of my bride, to postpone our marriage. She was only sixteen years old. I was to undertake a voyage of pleasure to beguile the time of expectation.

I hardly knew where to go. One of my sisters, who is settled in Paris, wished me to stay with her; a dear friend wanted to take me off to Spain. I finally resolved to go straight to Naples, to pass the winter at Malta for the benefit of my rather delicate health, and then to return home by way of the East. I even got letters of introduction for Constantinople. I set out around the end of November 1841, intending to return the following spring.

My departure was very melancholy. I left behind me my beloved bride, an uncle whose affection rested on me, sisters, brothers, nieces whose society was my most valued delight. I left also the industrial schools for poor Jews with which I was so much employed, and many friends who loved me. To set out alone on so long a voyage! But, said I to myself, perhaps God will send me some friend on the way.

Before leaving, I wished to sign a large number of receipts connected with the subscriptions to the Jewish industrial society. I dated them in advance, January 15 and, having written this date so many times, I became weary of it and said, as I laid down my pen, "God only knows where I shall be on January 15, and whether that day may not be the day of my death."

I also attended a meeting of several distinguished Jews that was to consider the reform of the worship of Judaism, to bring it more into harmony with the spirit of the age. I went to the meeting, at which everyone gave his opinion on the improvements suggested. There were as many opinions as persons present. There was a great deal of discussion. They took into account the convenience of men, the events of the times, the axioms of public opinion, all the ideas of modern civilization. Everything was thought of and pondered; only one was forgotten—the law of God. I cannot remember that the name of God was mentioned once, or that of Moses, or the existence of the Bible.

My own private opinion was that they should allow all religious forms to die quietly out—that they need not have recourse either to books or to men, but that everyone should be left free to express and practice his faith in his own fashion. The meeting broke up without coming to any decision.

Finally I set out. As I left Strasbourg I was disquieted by a thousand strange presentiments. When we stopped to change horses, I was roused from my reverie by cries of joy and the sound of music. It was a rustic wedding. The happy, noisy villagers were just emerging from the church. Flutes and fiddles were going vigorously; the crowd came around my carriage, as though to invite me to share their joy.

"It will be my turn soon," I exclaimed, and this thought restored my cheerfulness.

I spent some days at Marseilles, where my friends and relatives received me with open arms. I could hardly tear myself away from their elegant hospitality. And truly it takes an effort to leave France, when one leaves also a whole life of loving associations. Indeed, the sea itself seemed to oppose my departure. It rolled along its mighty waves to bar my progress.

But all these obstacles were swept away by the steamer that took me to Naples. I was soon able to enjoy the magnificent infinity above me and around me; but what struck me more than sea or sky was man, that frail creature who braves all dangers, and masters the elements themselves. My pride was loftier than the rolling waves, and more tenacious.

The boat touched at Civita Vecchia. As we entered the harbor the sound of cannon greeted us. I asked, with a spiteful curiosity, the motive of this warlike sound in the peaceful territory of the Pope. "It is the feast," I was told, "of the Conception of Mary." I shrugged my shoulders and would not land.

The next day we reached Naples. The sun was shining gloriously, and producing brilliant effects on the smoke of Vesuvius. Never had I been so dazzled by any scene of nature. I saw before me the reality of those glowing images of the heavens and the sea with which artists and poets had filled my imagination.

I stayed a month at Naples, that I might see and describe everything. I wrote bitter words against the religion and the priests, who seemed to me so out of keeping with that magnificent country. I wrote to Strasbourg that I had drunk some *lachryma Christi* on Vesuvius to the health of the Abbe Ratisbonne.

My betrothed wrote to ask me if I agreed with those who said, "See Naples and die." No, I replied, but see Naples and live; live to see it again.

I had no wish to go to Rome, although two friends of my family whom I often saw urged me strongly to do so—M. Coulman, a Protestant, and formerly deputy of Strasbourg, and Baron Rothschild, whose family lavished on me every kind of attention. I could not yield to their persuasions. My betrothed wished me to go directly to Malta, and she sent me a recommendation from my physician that I should spend the winter there, and carefully avoid Rome because of the malignant fevers which, he said, prevailed there.

These reasons would have prevented my going to Rome, even if I had placed that city on my original program.

M. Coulman had introduced me to an amiable and estimable man who was going to Malta. I was so pleased at this that I said, "This is surely the friend God has sent me."

I reserved my place in the *Mongibello* for Sicily. A friend accompanied me on board the vessel to purchase my ticket, and promised to return and bid me farewell before we started. He came, but did not find me.

Meanwhile, the first day of the new year arrived. It was a sad day to me. I thought of my family, of the festivity and joy with which my uncle always kept that day. The lively gaiety of the Neapolitans deepened my sadness. I went out, to shake off my melancholy, and followed the crowd mechanically. I reached the plaza in front of the palace, and found myself at the door of a church.

I went in. I think a priest was saying Mass. I remained there, leaning against a pillar, and my heart seemed to open in a new atmosphere. I prayed after my own fashion, without taking any notice of what was going on around me. I prayed for my betrothed, for my uncle, for my deceased father, for the loving mother who had been taken from me so early and for all who were dear to me; and I asked of God some inspiration, some hint of His will that might guide me in my projects for improving the condition of the Jews.

My sadness passed away, and my heart was filled with calm, such as I should have felt if a voice had said to me, "Your prayer is heard."

But how did I get to Rome?

I do not know, nor can I account for it in any way. I almost fancy I must have lost my way; for instead of going to the office of the Palermo boats, as I intended when I left my lodgings, I found myself in the office of the diligences for Rome. I told M. Vigne, the friend who was to accompany me to Malta, that I could not resist the temptation of making an expedition to Rome, but that I would certainly be back at Naples so as to leave with him on January 20. I left Naples on the fifth, and reached Rome on the sixth, the feast of the Epiphany. I had for my fellow traveler an Englishman named Marshall, whose original conversation amused me very much.

I was so pressed for time, that I eagerly devoured ruins like a thorough tourist. I filled my imagination and my journal with a confused medley of impressions. I visited with monotonous admiration all the innumerable magnificences of Rome. I was most frequently accompanied by my English friend, and by a guide. I have no notion what religion they were, for neither of them gave any sign of Christianity in the churches, and I believed I behaved far more reverently than they did.

On January 8, as I was going my round of sightseeing, I heard someone calling me in the street; it was my old friend Gustave de Bussieres. I was very happy to meet him. We went to dine with my friend's father, and in that agreeable circle I felt some measure of the joy with which one greets any memorial of one's own country in a strange land.

As I entered the drawing room Theodore de Bussieres, the eldest son of the family, was leaving it. I did not know him personally, but I knew that he was my brother's friend and namesake. I knew that he had deserted Protestantism and become a Catholic, and this was quite enough to inspire me with a profound antipathy to him. I fancied that this feeling was reciprocal. However, as Theodore de Bussieres was already well known for his published volume of travels in Sicily and in the East, I was very glad to ask him some questions before starting in that direction. Whether on that account, or from mere civility, I suggested that I pay him a visit. He answered very kindly, and added that he had just received a letter from my brother the abbe, and that he would give me his new address.

"I will gladly receive it," said I, "although I shall not need it."

When he had left, I felt annoyed at the obligation I had imposed on myself of making a useless visit and wasting my precious time.

I continued running about Rome all day long, except

two hours in the morning which I spent with Gustave; and in the evening I took my ease, either at the theater or at some party. My conversations with Gustave were very animated, for the meeting of two old schoolfellows furnishes an inexhaustible store of amusing and interesting memories. But he was a Protestant, with all the zeal and enthusiasm of the Pietists of Alsace. He talked largely of the superiority of his sect to all other Christian communities, and was very eager to convert me. I was much amused, as I had fancied that the mania of proselytism was peculiar to Catholics. I generally evaded his assaults by some merry jest, but once, to console him for the failure of his attempts, I promised him that if ever I took it into my head to be converted, I would turn Pietist. In return, he promised that he would be present at my marriage the following August.

All his efforts to detain me at Rome were ineffectual. Others of my friends, Edmund Humann and Alfred de Lotzbeck, joined him in begging me to remain in Rome for the carnival. But I could not consent. I feared I should grieve and distress my betrothed, and M. Vigne expected me at Naples in time to start with him on January 20.

I was making the best use of the short time that remained, and went to the Capitol to visit the Church of Aracoeli. The imposing appearance of that church, the solemn chants that were echoing along its vast nave, the historical recollections awakened by the ground I was treading—all combined to produce a profound impression on me. My guide, noticing that I was disturbed, told me he had frequently seen strangers affected in a similar way in that church.

As we came down from the Capitol, he led me through the Ghetto, the quarter assigned to the Jews. There I felt an emotion of an entirely different kind—mingled pity and indignation. What, I exclaimed, as I beheld that miserable sight, is this that Roman charity of which so much is said? In horror I asked myself whether a whole nation deserved to be the victims of such barbarous treatment and of such endless prejudices, simply for having killed one man eighteen hundred years ago.

I described all that I had seen for my family, and went back to the Capitol. The Church of Aracoeli was in a great bustle of preparation for some grand ceremony. I asked the reason for it, and was told that two Jews named Constantini, of Ancona, were going to be baptized. I cannot describe the indignation I felt on receiving this information. When my guide asked whether I should like to be present, I exclaimed, "What! *I* assist at so infamous a spectacle! No, no, I should not be able to restrain myself from making a desperate assault on both priests and victims."

I had never felt so fierce a hatred towards Christianity as after that visit to the Ghetto.

I had a few farewell visits to make, and my promise to Baron de Bussieres occurred to me continually as an awkward obligation. Most fortunately, I had not asked his address, and I resolved to make this circumstance my excuse for not performing my promise.

It was now the fifteenth, and I went to reserve my place for Naples. My departure was fixed for the seventeenth. I went next into a bookshop to look over some works on Constantinople. As I was coming out, I met a servant of M. de Bussieres senior, on the Corso. He saluted me in passing, and I stopped him to ask the address of Baron de Bussieres. Piazza Nicosia, he said, number 38.

And now, whether I liked it or not, I was committed

to this visit. I put it off to the last moment, and at length set off, carrying in my hand a card on which I had written *p.p.c.*[*] I found the Piazza Nicosia after many turns; number 38 was next door to the office at which I had reserved my place for Naples the same day.

My reception at the house of de Bussieres was annoying. Instead of simply taking my card, the servant suddenly announced me, and introduced me into the drawing room. I concealed my vexation as well as I could beneath a civil smile, and took a chair near Mme. De Bussieres, who was sitting with her two daughters.

Our conversation was at first very general, but it soon began to take a tone of passion, as I related my impressions of Rome. I looked on de Bussieres as an enthusiast, in the ill-natured sense of the word, and was very glad to have the opportunity to plague him about the Jews of Rome. It was a relief to me to do so; but my complaints of course led our conversation upon religious ground. De Bussieres spoke to me of the majesty and grandeur of Catholicism. I replied with irony, and with some of the many insults I had heard and read, although I checked my frenzy out of respect for Mme. de Bussieres and the two children.

"Well," said de Bussieres, "since you detest superstition, and profess yourself so very liberal about doctrine—since you are so enlightened—have you the courage to submit yourself to a very simple and innocent test?"

"What test?"

"Only to wear a little something I will give you. Look, it is a medal of the Blessed Virgin. It seems very ridiculous,

---

[*] *P.p.c., pour prendre conge,* to take leave, a customary note left on a calling card at the home of an acquaintance when leaving a town.

does it not? But I assure you I attach great value and efficacy to this little medal."

This proposal astonished me by its puerile oddity. My first impulse was to laugh and shrug my shoulders, but it struck me that this scene could furnish me a delicious chapter for my journal. I consented to take the medal, so that I could show it as a confirmation of the story. The medal was passed around my neck, not without difficulty, for the ribbon was rather short, but at length we succeeded.

"Ha, ha!" I exclaimed with a hearty laugh, "Here I am, a Catholic, apostolic and Roman!"

De Bussieres showed a childlike pleasure in his victory, and hastened to push his advantage.

"Now," said he, "you must perfect the test. You must say every night and morning the Memorare, a very short and very efficacious prayer which St. Bernard addressed to the Blessed Virgin Mary."

"What do you mean with your Memorare?" I exclaimed. "Come, let us have done with this folly."

The name of St. Bernard reminded me of my brother, who had written a life of that saint. I had never read his book, but the association rekindled all my antipathy to proselytism, Jesuitism and all those I called hypocrites and apostates.

I begged de Bussieres to drop the subject, and I said, with a smile of contempt, that I regretted not having a Hebrew prayer to offer him in return, but I had not one, and could not recollect one.

He persisted, however. He said that by refusing to recite the prayer I made the test useless, and that I proved thereby the reality of the willful obstinacy with which the Jews were reproached. I did not wish to attach too much importance to the matter, and so I said, "Well, then, I promise to say this prayer. If it does me no good, it cannot do me any harm."

And de Bussieres went to look for it, and gave it to me, begging me to copy it for him. I consented, on the condition that I might keep the original, and give him my copy. I planned to enrich my journal with this additional piece of evidence.

And now we were both satisfied. Our conversation seemed to me very whimsical and amusing. I took my departure, and spent the evening at the theater, thinking no more either of my medal or of the Memorare.

But when I came home I found a note from de Bussieres, who had called to return my visit, begging me to see him once more before I left Rome. I had to return his Memorare, and as I was to leave in the morning, I packed my trunks and then sat down to copy the prayer. *Memorare, O piissima Virgo.*

The next day, January 16, I got my passport signed and completed all my preparations, but as I walked along I could not help repeating the words of the Memorare. How was it that those words had taken so deep a hold on my mind? I could not put them away. I said them over and over, just as one hums a tune which haunts one, without conscious effort.

About eleven I called on de Bussieres, to return to him his tenacious and peremptory prayer. I talked to him about my proposed travels in the East, and he gave me much excellent advice.

"But," he said suddenly, "it is strange that you persist in leaving Rome at the very time when people are coming from all parts for the great ceremonies at St. Peter's. Perhaps you will never have the chance again, and you will be sorry to have missed an opportunity which so many seek with eager curiosity."

I replied that my place was reserved and paid for, that I had written to inform my family of my departure, that I expected letters at Palermo, that it was now too late to change my plans and that my mind was made up. Our conversation was interrupted by the postman, who brought a letter from my brother, the Abbe Ratisbonne. He showed me the letter, but it was quite devoid of interest to me, as it related to a book he was publishing in Paris. My brother did not know I was in Rome, but this unexpected episode threatened to close my visit, as I was eager to avoid everything that could remind me of him.

Nevertheless I was induced, incomprehensibly, to prolong my stay at Rome. I granted to the urgency of a man I hardly knew what I had obstinately refused to my most intimate friends.

What was that impulse that led me to do what I had so firmly resolved not to do? Was it not a continuation of the same force that had brought me from Strasbourg to Italy despite my tempting invitation to Paris?—that led me from Naples to Rome in spite of my firm determination to go straight to Sicily?—that at Rome compelled me, on the eve of my departure, to pay a visit that annoyed me?

I had received the name of Tobias along with that of Alphonse. I had quite forgotten my name, but the unseen angel had not forgotten me. He was the friend God had sent me, although I knew him not. How many there are in the world who know not the guides of their journeys!

I had no wish to spend the carnival in Rome, but I did wish to see the Pope. De Bussieres had assured me I should see him very soon at St. Peter's. Meanwhile we took several rambles together. We talked over everything we saw—monuments, pictures, manners and customs; but religion contrived to mix itself with everything. De Bussieres introduced it with such simplicity, and enforced it with so keen and ardent a zeal, that I said to myself that if anything could disgust a man with religion it was the importunity with which his conversion was sought. My natural gaiety led me to turn the most serious subjects to ridicule, and the light flashes of my fancy often deepened into blasphemy.

And yet de Bussieres was uniformly calm and indulgent. He even said once, "In spite of your rage, I have a sure conviction that you will be a Christian one day, for there is in you a groundwork of rectitude which comforts me when I think of you, and persuades me that you will be enlightened, even though an angel from Heaven be needed for that end."

"Ha, well and good," said I, "for otherwise the matter would not be easy to manage."

As we passed the Scala Santa, de Bussieres was seized with a fit of enthusiasm. He rose in the carriage, uncovered his head and said in a tone of fervor, "Hail, Scala Santa! Here is a sinner who will one day climb you on his knees!"

It would be completely impossible to express the effect produced upon me by this unexpected and extraordinary honor paid to some old steps. I laughed at it as something hopelessly, grotesquely mad. A short time later, as we drove through the charming gardens of the Villa Wolkonski, I rose and exclaimed, "Hail, true marvels of God's power! It is before you that I kneel in homage, and not before an old staircase!"

We went out again on the two following days. On the nineteenth, I saw de Bussieres again, but he seemed sad and dejected. I withdrew out of delicacy, without inquiring the cause of his sadness.

I was to leave on the twenty-second, for I had again reserved a place for Naples. De Bussieres' engagements seemed to have diminished his zeal for my conversion, and I fancied he had forgotten all about his miraculous medal. Still I kept muttering to myself, though with great impatience, that everlasting, importunate invocation of St. Bernard.

In the middle of the night before January 20, I awoke suddenly and saw before me a large black cross, of a peculiar form, and without the figure of Christ. I made many attempts to get rid of the image, but I could not succeed; however I turned, there it was before me. I fell asleep at length; and when I awoke in the morning I thought no more about it.

If anyone had said to me that morning, "You have risen a Jew; you will lie down a Christian," I should have looked on him as hopelessly, ludicrously mad.

That morning, Thursday, after having taken breakfast at my hotel and carried my letters to the post, I went to call on my friend Gustave, the Pietist, who had just returned from a shooting excursion which had taken him for some days from Rome. He was surprised to see me still in Rome; I told him my motive for remaining was to see the Pope.

"But I shall leave without seeing him after all," I said, "for he took no part in the ceremony of the *Cathedra Petri*, although I had been led to hope he would do so."

Gustave consoled me by speaking of another ceremony, and a very curious one, he said, which was to take place, I think, at Santa Maria Maggiore. He alluded to a blessing of animals; and thereupon followed a shower of jests and sarcasms, just as you can imagine a Jew and a Protestant would utter.

We parted about eleven, after making an appointment for the next day to see a picture which had been commissioned for our friend Baron de Lotzbeck. I went off to a café in the Piazza di Spagna to read the newspapers. I had just entered when Edmund Humann sat down at my side, and we talked very gaily about Paris, and the fine arts and politics. Soon Alfred de Lotzbeck accosted me; with him I held an even more frivolous conversation. We talked of hunting, of all kinds of pleasures, of the mirth of the carnival, of the brilliant soiree given the evening before by the Duke de Torlonia. Nor did we forget the festivities of my approaching marriage, to which I invited him; he promised to be there.

If at that moment—it was noon—a third person had come up to me, and had said, "Alphonse, in a quarter of an hour you will be adoring Jesus Christ, your God and your Savior; you will be prostrate in a poor church; you will be smiting your breast at the feet of a priest in a convent of Jesuits, where you will spend the carnival in preparing for your baptism; and you will feel ready to offer yourself in sacrifice for the Catholic faith; you will renounce the world, its pomps, its pleasures; your fortune, your hopes, your bright glad future; and if necessary, you will renounce your betrothed also, and the love of your family, the esteem of your friends, the attachment of the Jews; and you will have but one aspiration, to follow Jesus Christ, and to bear His cross even unto death"—I say that if some prophet had spoken before me a prediction like this, I should have thought that there could be only one man more mad than he, the man who could believe in the possibility of anything so absurd. And yet it is this absurdity and folly which now compose my wisdom and my happiness.

The Conversion of Ratisbonne

As I left the café, I met de Bussieres. He asked me to wait a few minutes at the Church of San Andrea delle Fratte, which was close by, as he had some business there. They were busy with preparations for a funeral, and I inquired the name of the person for whom these honors were intended.

"It is one of my friends," de Bussieres replied, "Count de Laferronnays. His sudden death is the cause of the depression of spirits you may have observed in me the last day or two."

I did not know de Laferronnays, I had never even seen him; and so I felt nothing more than that vague sorrow one always feels at hearing of a sudden death. De Bussieres went to arrange for the gallery that was to be set apart for the family of the deceased.

"I shall not tax your patience long," said he. "I shall not be away more than a few minutes."

The Church of San Andrea delle Fratte is small and poor; at that hour it was almost deserted. I think I was almost the only person in it, and there was no work of art to attract my attention. I was looking around mechanically, without any definite thought or purpose; I remember only a black dog, which bounded and jumped before me as I moved about. Suddenly the dog disappeared. The whole church disappeared; I saw nothing further. Or rather, O my God, I saw only one object!

And how should I speak of it? No words of man can even attempt to utter the unutterable. All description, however sublime, must be only a degradation of the ineffable reality.

I lay prostrate, my heart completely absorbed and lost, when de Bussieres recalled me to life. I could not answer his questions, but I grasped my medal and kissed the image of the Virgin, radiant with grace. It was indeed her very self.

I knew that de Laferronnays had prayed for me. I cannot tell how I knew it, any more than I can account for the truths of which I had suddenly gained both the knowledge and the belief. All I can say is that at the moment when the Blessed Virgin made a sign with her hand, the veil fell from my eyes; not one veil only, but all the veils that were wrapped around me disappeared, just as snow melts beneath the rays of the sun.

I came out of a tomb, out of an abyss, and I was living, perfectly, energetically living. And yet I wept. I saw before me the fearful miseries from which I had been rescued by the mercy of God. I thought of my brother with joy—but the rest of my family, my betrothed, my sisters! Are you never to raise your eyes to the Savior of the world, whose blood has washed away original sin? O, how foul is the blot of that stain! How completely it obliterates every trace by which we might recognize the creature that was made in the image of God!

I am asked how I attained a knowledge of these truths, since it is well known that I never opened a religious book and had never read a page of the Bible, and that the dogma of original sin, which is either denied or forgotten by modern Jews, had never for a single moment occupied my thoughts—indeed, I doubt I had ever heard its name. How did I arrive at a knowledge of it? I know not. All I know is that when I entered that church I was profoundly ignorant of everything, and that when I came out I saw everything clearly and distinctly. I was like a man suddenly roused from slumber, or rather like a man born blind, whose eyes are suddenly opened. He sees indeed, but he can give no definition of the light in which he beholds the objects around him.

The Conversion of Ratisbonne

I implored my confessor, Fr. de Villefort, and also de Bussieres, to observe secrecy in regard to what had happened to me. My earnest wish was to bury myself in a Trappist monastery, to occupy myself exclusively with the things of eternity and to find refuge from a world which could no longer understand me. I confess I thought my family and friends would consider me insane, that they would turn me to ridicule, that it was better in every way for me to escape from the world, from its opinions and its judgments.

However, my ecclesiastical superiors showed me that ridicule, reproach and false judgments were but a part of the chalice which is offered to every real Christian. They urged me not to decline this chalice, and told me how Jesus Christ had predicted suffering for His disciples. These solemn words increased my joy. I felt myself prepared for everything, and eagerly wished for Baptism. They wished to interpose some delay.

"But," I exclaimed, "the Jews who heard the preaching of the apostles were baptized immediately, and you wish to put me off, after I have seen the Queen of Apostles!"

They consoled me with the promise of an early baptism.

What kindness was lavished on me during the days of preparation! I was admitted into the house of the Jesuits, to make a retreat under Fr. de Villefort's direction. That man of God can hardly be called a man; he is rather a personification of charity. But no sooner were my eyes opened, than I saw around me many men of similar stamp, of whose existence the world knows nothing. I found wonderful kindness and delicacy in my first conversations with these Christians. The venerable superior of the Jesuits visited me every evening.

He spoke to me only a few words, but they were words that expanded as I listened to them, and filled me with joy and light and life.

O Rome, what grace and blessings I have found in you! The Mother of my Lord arranged all that concerned me. She brought a French priest to address me in my mother tongue at the moment of my baptism—the Abbe Dupanloup. The echoes of his mighty address which the press has repeated can give no idea of what it really was.

One further consolation was in reserve for me. You remember how earnestly I wished to see the Holy Father; indeed this desire, or this curiosity, had kept me at Rome longer than I intended. Little did I imagine under what circumstances my wish was to be gratified. As a newborn child of the Church I was presented to the Father of all the faithful. From the moment of my baptism I had felt for the Pope the reverent love of a son; and I was delighted when it was told to me that I was to be introduced into his presence by the general of the Jesuits. Yet I trembled, for the earth's greatest men fade into insignificance in the presence of this true greatness.

All the royalties of the earth seemed to me concentrated upon the head of the man who wields on earth the powers of the world to come, who succeeds in an unbroken line to the keys of St. Peter, and to the priesthood of Aaron—the representative of Jesus Christ Himself, whose unshaken throne he fills.

Never shall I forget my awe as I entered the Vatican, and passed through the courts and halls which lead to the sanctuary of the Pontiff. But all my anxiety was dispelled, to make room for surprise and wonder, when I saw him himself, so simple, so humble, so paternal. He was not a mon-

The Conversion of Ratisbonne

arch, but a father, whose extreme kindness treated me as a beloved son.

The letters I have received from my family set me free from every engagement. I offer my liberty to God, for all my life, to be employed in the service of the Church and of my brethren, under the protection of Mary.

Epilogue

As Alphonse Ratisbonne had foreseen, his uncle disinherited him, and revoked his partnership in the bank. In the year following his conversion, his brother Abbe Theodore Ratisbonne helped him to found the Sisterhood of Our Lady of Sion to work for the conversion of Jews. In 1847 he was ordained a priest, and joined the Jesuits. In 1855, with the approval of Pius IX, he left the Jesuits and brought the Sisters of Sion to Jerusalem. There he built the large Convent of Ecce Homo, with a school and an orphanage for girls. A few years later he added a church, another convent and another girls' orphanage at Ain Karim, and an orphanage for boys outside Jerusalem, with a school of mechanical arts. The Peres de Notre Dame de Sion, the priests who came to help him in the Holy Land, also established foundations back in Europe. Sixty years after Ratisbonne's death at Ain Karim, these priests were among the most active and intrepid rescuers of Jews from the Nazis.

Appendix

From Abbe Omer Englebert, *Catherine Laboure and the Modern Miracles of Our Lady*, P.J. Kennedy & Sons, New York, 1959, translated by Alastair Guinan:

The Church is usually cautious about a conversion, for the reason that no one can be certain of the future role of the convert, especially if he be young and in good health. Nevertheless, the events of January 20 aroused so much interest at Rome and in France that a Roman court of inquiry was immediately convened. The hearings lasted until June 3, at which time a pontifical decree was published stating "that it is certain that a true and notable miracle, the work of God, through the intercession of the Blessed Virgin, did produce the instantaneous and complete conversion of Alphonse Ratisbonne."

These are the same terms that the breviary was to take up and incorporate into the Office of the Miraculous Medal. As we have seen, the conversion was instantaneous; what is to follow will show it to have been complete.

"Letters of my family left me at liberty to do as I wished," Alphonse wrote on April 12, 1842. In other words, he lost his inheritance, and he was denied by his own; he lost, as well, his fiancee, and in addition he saw her who had been a deist turn again into an atheist.

In June 1842, the same month in which the Roman decree was published, he entered the Society of Jesus. Here he remained for six years. Finally, he withdrew from the Jesuits in order to join his brother Theodore in the foundation of the Congregation of the Priests and Dames of Sion. Their work was to be the conversion of the Jews.

The Conversion of Ratisbonne

The two brothers divided the world responsibility between them: to the older was assigned the care of the West and the establishment of institutions in France, in England, in Austria and in Romania; to the younger was given the Orient, together with Constantinople and the Holy Places. He who had been favored with the apparition of Our Lady in St. Andrea delle Fratte was now Pere Marie-Alphonse, and he acquired the ruins of the praetorium of Pontius Pilate and made three foundations in Jerusalem: the Ecce Homo, St. John in Montana and the College of St. Peter.

He was in need of funds to support these foundations, and out of love for his fellow Jews, the one-time dandy became a beggar. He was himself typically Jewish in appearance, and as he went about with his long beard he seemed like some high priest of the Old Law. He was always merry and kind, and he gave generously to all of his own interior happiness as he sought to obtain their charity.

For many years he traveled through Spain, France, Belgium, England, Austria and Germany. At times he was well received, at others harshly rebuffed. In London he was once invited to attend a party with the promise that he would encounter many generous people who would be interested in his work. He found that it was into the center of a ballroom that he had been taken, and there they mocked him. While in Paris he was summoned before the archbishop's officials as being suspected of soliciting funds for a non-existent sanctuary.

He was endowed with the directness of a child and with remarkable humility. One day he asked his great friend Pere Estrade, "Can you understand why it was that the Virgin appeared to a being like myself, and why it was to me

From Abbé Omer Englebert

that she pointed out the congregation which her divine Son wished to see established?"

Pere Estrade rose and looked directly at Ratisbonne.

"Yes, I understand it," he said.

"Do you know *why?*"

"Why? It was because in choosing an instrument as unworthy as yourself she knew that naught of the glory due to God would be deflected upon the instrument; that all glory would return to the Author of all good."

"Ah," said Pere Marie-Alphonse delightedly, "this is a point of view that had escaped me. I will take care not to forget it."

On the details of the miracle he remained reserved and mysterious. Following the canonical inquiry, it was only to the Comte de Chambord,* to Pere Estrade and to two or three intimate friends that he ever spoke of the vision. His friend Mere Stouhlen, foundress of the Dames of Sion, said to him on one occasion, "I should like to ask you a question. Will you answer it?"

"Gladly."

"Do you still see the Blessed Virgin?"

"She is more and more lovely," he said; and then he bowed his head.

He was even more reticent on the subject of the interior trials from which he suffered so long and so bitterly. Yet we know that he did drink the chalice of tribulation which had been predicted to him, and that the great cross which was shown to him on the night of January 20 was grievous to bear.

---

* The Comte de Chambord (1820-1883), grandson of Charles X and pretender to the throne of France, was the last of the French Bourbons.

The Conversion of Ratisbonne

On May 6, 1884 he died. His last words, "All my wishes have been granted!" were spoken in response to someone who had asked him how he felt.

Did Our Lady manifest herself to him at that last moment? According to those who watched by him, "at about eight o'clock in the evening, a light shone upon his face, and he opened his eyes, which had been hitherto continually closed. They seemed full of life, and they expressed at first surprise and then delight. This appearance of ecstasy lasted for three minutes. Then he gently dropped his lids and effortlessly and quietly gave up his soul to God. He seemed to be peacefully asleep, and it was a long while before any sign of death appeared upon his face."

And what of his little fiancée, the girl of sixteen so fearful of the effects of the Roman climate on her future husband, and whom he had promised, as she went from him, that he would keep ever in her prayers and would ever hope for their reunion in Heaven?

Although the conversion of Alphonse was, as the Roman Breviary says, "instantaneous," that of Flore required more time. As we learn from Abbe Klein's book on Madeleine Semer,[*] time ran on for three-quarters of a century. On October 30, 1912, Madeleine Semer, a young divorcee who had been married to a prominent member of the French Chamber of Deputies, was in search of employment in Paris. She applied to an elderly woman who engaged her as a secretary and reader, and who soon came to treat her as a friend.

Madame Singer, formerly Flore Ratisbonne, was then in her 88th year. She had retained all the brilliance of mind

---

[*] Felix Klein, *Madeleine Semer, convertie et mystique, 1874-1921*. 28th ed. (Paris, 1929).

From Abbe Omer Englebert

and the goodness of heart that had won her so many friends. In the days of the Second Empire such figures as Prevost-Paradol, Octave Feuillet, Caro and Emile Ollivier had been among those who came to her home. It was still a focus of noted visitors in 1912, and their stature had in no way lessened. Now the guests included Brunetiere, Paul Deschanel and Prince Albert de Monaco, and they visited her regularly.* It was at Madame Singer's that Madeleine Semer discussed philosophical matters with Bergson and set out upon that path of development which brought her soul from unbelief to Christian mysticism.

Madame Singer herself was always held back by the problem of evil: its existence kept her from believing in God. In her words of leave-taking to Madeleine Semer, as they are found in her will, we read these suggestions of atheism: "You are well aware of my limited budget, and you know, my very dear friend, that I am not able to cover you with gold as you indeed deserve. But I yet feel that the life-long gratitude I feel toward you will be truly valued by you. In the most considerate and most consistent fashion you have unfailingly been at my side to help me bear my constant sufferings. If

---

* Prevost-Paradol (1829-1870), writer and journalist. Napoleon III had hopes of securing the intervention of the United States in the War of 1870 on the side of France, and he sent Prevost-Paradol to Washington to this end; but he committed suicide at the French Embassy shortly after his arrival there. Octave Feuillet (1821-1890), novelist and playwright. Elme-Marie Caro (1826-1887), philosopher and moralist. Emile Ollivier (1825-1913), son-in-law of Liszt and brother-in-law of Wagner, he was President of the Council of State in France at the time of the War of 1870. Ferdinand Brunetiere (1849-1906), literary critic. Paul Deschanel (1885-1922), President of the French Republic. Prince Albert of Monaco (1848-1922), a distinguished expert in oceanography. Henri Bergson (1851-1944), a philosopher of Polish antecedents who became a naturalized Frenchman.

you have not been able to win me to belief in God, Father of all mankind, I nevertheless do believe in his angels; for you have been a slave to duty and an angel of mercy."

However, when Madame Singer finally died on November 25, 1915, she had been in the habit for three months of asking Madeleine Semer to recite the evening prayer aloud in her presence each night. And on the last night of her life, while perfectly lucid, she declared that all her objections to God's Providence had faded away. Three times she asked her friend to say the Lord's Prayer with her.

DECREE VERIFYING AND ACCREDITING THE MIRACLE

In the name of God, amen.

In the year of our Lord and Savior Jesus Christ one thousand eight hundred and forty-two, being the fifteenth of the Roman indiction and the twelfth year of the pontificate of our Holy Father Pope Gregory XVI, and on the third day of June.

In the presence of the Very Eminent and Reverend Constantine Cardinal Patrizi, Vicar General of our Holy Father the Pope, ordinary judge of the Roman Court, appeared the Very Reverend Francis Anivitti, Proctor-fiscal of the Tribune of the Vicariate, who had been specially deputed by the Very Eminent and Reverend Cardinal Vicar to make inquiry and to examine witnesses in regard to the truth and reality of the wonderful conversion from Judaism to the Catholic religion granted, through the intercession of the Blessed Virgin Mary, to Alphonse Ratisbonne, twenty-eight years of age, and now resident in this city: Proctor declares that he applied himself to the inquiry entrusted to him with the utmost diligence, and with a ready and willing mind. He declares further, that he has submitted the witnesses, to the number of nine, to a formal examination, and that they all display a marvelous agreement in their account of the alleged fact, and of its consequences and results. Whereupon he declared that, in his judgment, nothing was wanting in the characteristics of a true miracle; but that, nevertheless, he referred the decision of the question to his Eminence, and besought him to issue a definitive decree, as it might seem to him expedient in the Lord, after a full examination of the acts and documents laid before him.

Whereupon the Very Eminent and Reverend Cardinal Vicar, having received the report, and read the questions proposed to the witnesses, together with their answers, and after mature and careful consideration of the same, after having also taken the advice and judgment of theologians and other holy men, in the form required by the Council of Trent, Session 25, *de invocatione,* etc., pronounced and declared definitively that he affirmed the reality and truth of the miracle wrought by God, at the intercession of the Blessed Virgin Mary, in the instantaneous and perfect conversion from Judaism of Alphonse Ratisbonne aforesaid. And inasmuch as it is honorable to confess and reveal the works of God, his Eminence is please to permit that this narrative be printed and published, and held as authentic, for the glory of God, and for increasing the devotion of all true Christians to the Blessed Virgin Mary.

Given at the palace of the aforesaid Very Eminent and Reverend Cardinal Vicar and ordinary judge, on the day, month, and year aforesaid.

C. Card. Vicar
Cam. Diamilla, Notary
Joseph, Chancellor
Tarnassi, Secretary

Roman guides have observed that the Church of Aracoeli makes a profound impression on even sophisticated tourists—Ratisbonne among them

The evening after he first met Ratisbonne, Baron Théodore de Bussières went to watch before the Blessed Sacrament at the Church of Sts. Cosmas and Damian (to the right of central columns, with bell tower)

The frescoes of St. Stefano Rotundo depict "in terrible detail" the sufferings of the early martyrs. Ratisbonne was briefly impressed

The Church declared Ratisbonne's conversion, at the Church of St. Andrea delle Fratte, a direct intervention of Heaven—a miracle

The man who had hated the Jesuits was baptized at their principal church, the Gesu